EXPRESSIONS

An Inspirational Journey
through Poetry, Art, and Journaling

Ann C.K. Nickell

100th Man
Publishing

Expressions
by Ann C.K. Nickell

© 2023 by Ann C.K. Nickell

Published by
100th Man Publishing
424 Clay Avenue, #32621
Waco, TX 76703
www.100thmanpublishing.com

Printed in the United States of America.

Dedicated to my Mom and Dad

*Two wonderful people whom God brought
to this earth to bless all who knew them.*

Love You More

The World Belongs to You

Reach out into the unknown,
Your dreams are waiting there.
Tuck away all your fear,
It won't take you anywhere.

Open your mind to adventure,
Prepare for what's in store.
Traverse a forgotten road,
Walk through the open door.

Ready yourself for battle,
Slip on your armored suit.
Shield your heart from doubters,
Their dread can take root.

Learn to believe in magic,
It touches everything.
Always believe in yourself,
You can do or be anything.

You can have all that you wish,
Your heart's every desire.
The world belongs to you,
Blaze a trail and set it on fire.

THE WORLD BELONGS TO

JOURNAL

JOURNAL

_____
_____
_____
_____
_____
_____
_____
_____
_____
_____
_____
_____
_____
_____
_____
_____
_____
_____
_____
_____
_____
_____
_____
_____
_____
_____

The War Inside

The wind rustled her hair as she walked along the shore.
Her smile hid the fact that inside her raged a war.

She walked to and fro, moving along with the tide.
The sounds of the ocean helped heal the pain inside.

She stopped for a few moments and stared into the abyss.
And wondered, if the ocean took her, would she be missed.

STARED INTO THE

ABYSS

JOURNAL

JOURNAL

_____
_____
_____
_____
_____
_____
_____
_____
_____
_____
_____
_____
_____
_____
_____
_____
_____
_____
_____
_____
_____
_____
_____
_____
_____
_____

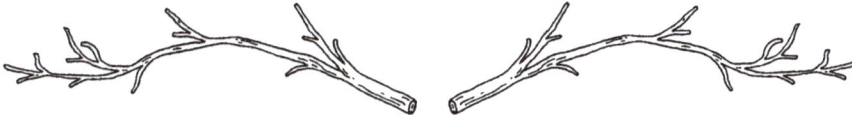

Rain

Standing alone in the rain, staring up at the sky.
The drops mingle with my tears, hiding that I cry.

The water rushes over me, washing away my pain.
Leaving me clean and open to all I have to gain.

The rain stops, the clouds part, the sun peeking through.
The light reveals my spirit, alive, refreshed and new.

WASHING
AWAY MY PAIN

JOURNAL

JOURNAL

Home

Traveling through the forest
guided by the light of the moon.
I follow my lonely heart home,
follow it back to you.

A path of glistening leaves
rustles in welcome beneath my feet.
A gurgling stream serenades me
as a cool breeze caresses my cheek.

A family of deer accompany me
as I wind my way through the pines.
Their hearts call out to each other
as yours calls out to mine.

I feel as though I belong here,
for the rhythm matches my own.
I am wrapped in light and love
as the forest guides me home.

THE FOREST GUIDES ME HOME

JOURNAL

_____

_____

_____

_____

_____

_____

_____

_____

_____

_____

_____

_____

_____

_____

_____

_____

_____

_____

_____

_____

_____

_____

_____

_____

JOURNAL

_____

_____

_____

_____

_____

_____

_____

_____

_____

_____

_____

_____

_____

_____

_____

_____

_____

_____

_____

_____

_____

_____

_____

_____

Spirits

The spirits awake and gather here,
remnants of an ancient past.

They frolic and play in the moonlight,
enjoying the spell that was cast.

It awoke their long lost memories
of happiness, love, and sorrow.

They play like movies of their lives,
but fade upon the morrow.

For daylight broke the eerie spell
and the spirits have all fled.

This world belongs to the living
to enjoy until they're dead.

THE SPIRITS AWAKE

JOURNAL

JOURNAL

_____
_____
_____
_____
_____
_____
_____
_____
_____
_____
_____
_____
_____
_____
_____
_____
_____
_____
_____
_____
_____
_____
_____
_____

Lost and Forgotten

She lost her life today, her blood staining the cold floor.
The sharp blade caught his reflection as he ran out the door.
She had no other family, no friends with whom she shared.
Her life will be forgotten because no one cared.

He lost his life today, his body broken and bruised.
His last sight of bloody knuckles, the only weapon they used.
Tossed like trash on the street, that is where he slowly died.
No one told his story, as a single loved one cried.

I lost my life today, my last sense the crushing sound.
The man behind the wheel stayed late for one more round.
The scene will be cleared tomorrow, the media will be gone.
My life will be forgotten as everyone moves on.

We lost our lives today, but no one knows our names.
We died alone so the media ignored our killers' shame.
We lost our lives today, by car, by knife, by hand.
Our lives weren't taken by bullets, so no one took a stand.

A SINGLE
LOVED ONE
CRIED

JOURNAL

_____

_____

_____

_____

_____

_____

_____

_____

_____

_____

_____

_____

_____

_____

_____

_____

_____

_____

_____

_____

_____

_____

JOURNAL

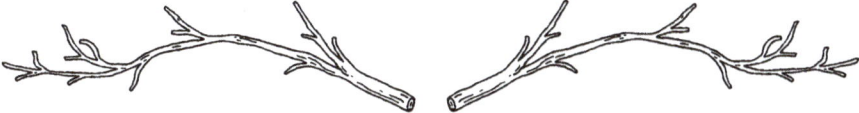

Hope

Sometimes the days are long, and you feel all hope is lost.
You push yourself to get ahead, no matter what it might cost.

Others talk you down, and you fall, losing sight of your dreams.
One day you realize that their world is not as great as it seems.

It's never too late to follow your heart, to go your own way.
The sun will always rise, bringing with it a brand new day.

THE SUN WILL ALWAYS

RISE

JOURNAL

_____

_____

_____

_____

_____

_____

_____

_____

_____

_____

_____

_____

_____

_____

_____

_____

_____

_____

_____

_____

_____

_____

_____

_____

_____

_____

_____

JOURNAL

Never Count Me Out

I may have been behind the others
and took some time to start.

I tripped and stumbled along the way
as my life was torn apart.

I may have trudged along at the bottom
with the world holding me down.

I believed the slander of the enemy
and fell and lost my crown.

I fought with light through the darkness
and triumphed over the doubt.

I am rising from the dust and ashes
so never count me out.

FELL AND LOST MY CROWN

JOURNAL

_____

_____

_____

_____

_____

_____

_____

_____

_____

_____

_____

_____

_____

_____

_____

_____

_____

_____

_____

_____

_____

_____

_____

_____

JOURNAL

Nightmare

Lost in an eerie nightmare, frightened, cold and alone.
I fight to escape the darkness, but my will is not my own.

The monsters all surround me, forcing me into their snare.
I search to find a way out, but there are traps everywhere.

I slip and stumble into a hole, and fall far into the deep.
Where villains rule, demons dwell, and beasts like to creep.

The ear piercing roaring makes it hard for me to think.
I'm handed a bottle of poison, and I tilt my head to drink.

The howling rushes over me as I crumple to the ground.
The lights dim, and the noise fades, until there is no sound.

Only my barely beating heart, fighting until the very end.
When my last breath leaves my body, I watch my soul ascend.

WHERE BEASTS LIKE TO CREEP

JOURNAL

_____

_____

_____

_____

_____

_____

_____

_____

_____

_____

_____

_____

_____

_____

_____

_____

_____

_____

_____

_____

_____

JOURNAL

_____

_____

_____

_____

_____

_____

_____

_____

_____

_____

_____

_____

_____

_____

_____

_____

_____

_____

_____

_____

_____

_____

_____

_____

The Boy from the Sea

Shrouded in mystery
Swept in by the sea
They called him outcast
He considered it free

Our eyes met at sunset
It was meant to be
He had not much to give
But he offered it to me

No one understood us
But all could agree
That we both were lost
As he knelt on one knee

Our hearts now entwined
He swept me to the sea
We basked in our love
The mystery boy and me

HE SWEPT ME TO THE SEA

JOURNAL

JOURNAL

America

Welcome to America, the Statue of Liberty cried.
Welcome to the country where your forefathers lived and died.

Welcome to freedom, I hope it treats you well.
Welcome to liberty, hear the ringing of the bell.

Welcome to opportunity, look for chances along the way.
Welcome to prosperity, if you work hard every day.

Welcome to life and love, do all you wish to do.
Welcome to your dreams, may all of them come true.

WELCOME TO AMERICA

JOURNAL

JOURNAL

_____
_____
_____
_____
_____
_____
_____
_____
_____
_____
_____
_____
_____
_____
_____
_____
_____
_____
_____
_____
_____
_____
_____
_____
_____
_____

Image

I can't look at myself in the mirror, can't look myself in the eye.
I believed that I was loved, but that love was all a lie.

I'm no longer wanted or needed, I don't fill my mate with desire.
What used to fan the flames, no longer sparks the fire.

I am filled with hate and self-loathing, as dark and blue as the sky.
Romance that once made me smile, now makes me cry.

I am alone in the world with nothing left but my name.
So I lock myself away to hide my pain and my shame.

HIDE MY PAIN AND MY SHAME

JOURNAL

_____
_____
_____
_____
_____
_____
_____
_____
_____
_____
_____
_____
_____
_____
_____
_____
_____
_____
_____
_____
_____
_____
_____

JOURNAL

True Love

You are the wind that fills my sails, pushing me along.
When my soul can't find the music, you sing me a new song.

When all my dreams are lost, you give me one of yours.
You help me find a window when there are no open doors.

You laugh with me when I'm happy, cry with me when I'm blue.
You are the greatest person I know, and my heart belongs to you.

TRUE LOVE

JOURNAL

_____
_____
_____
_____
_____
_____
_____
_____
_____
_____
_____
_____
_____
_____
_____
_____
_____
_____
_____
_____
_____
_____
_____
_____
_____
_____
_____

JOURNAL

New Journey

Floating off on the calm sea, pulled out by the tide.
Starting a new adventure with the stars as my guide.

The only sound is the water flowing past the hull.
There is no need for light for the moon is bright and full.

I am on this journey alone, but I am not afraid.
I laid out a plan and bowed my head and prayed.

The wind lifts my hair and cools the salt on my skin.
Happiness overcomes me, and I cannot help but grin.

I am free of the chains that held me for so long.
I am ready to write my own story and sing my own song.

STARTING A NEW ADVENTURE

JOURNAL

JOURNAL

_____
_____
_____
_____
_____
_____
_____
_____
_____
_____
_____
_____
_____
_____
_____
_____
_____
_____
_____
_____
_____
_____
_____
_____
_____

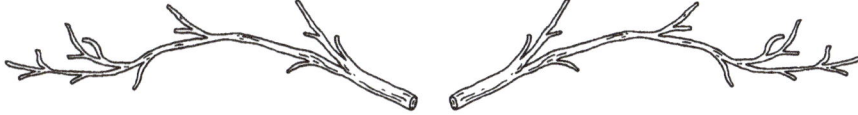

The Girl in the Box

The girl in the box cried out for help, but no one heard her voice.
They looked past her, unaware, distracted by their own noise.

Her tears ran freely, splashing around her, slowly filling the void.
Drowning all of her memories of the things she once enjoyed.

Her heart shattered inside her chest, each shard as sharp as a knife.
Cutting away at what was left of her torn and tattered life.

Hopelessness consumed her soul, turning it black as night.
Allowing the tendrils of death to creep in, extinguishing her light.

HER HEART SHATTERED

JOURNAL

_____
_____
_____
_____
_____
_____
_____
_____
_____
_____
_____
_____
_____
_____
_____
_____
_____
_____
_____
_____
_____
_____
_____
_____

JOURNAL

_____

_____

_____

_____

_____

_____

_____

_____

_____

_____

_____

_____

_____

_____

_____

_____

_____

_____

_____

_____

_____

_____

_____

_____

_____

_____

_____

Held

I'm frightened, Father
      I know, child
Help me
      Hold on tight
I'm losing touch
      Stay with me
I'm falling
      Don't give up
I'm frightened
      Don't be afraid
I'm sad
      You're not alone
I can't go on
      But I'm with you
I'm dying
      I won't let you
But no one cares
      I do
They laugh at me
      I don't
I don't fit in
      I include you
I'm a misfit
      You're just like me
I want to cry
      Then go ahead
Will anyone see
      Only me
No one will hold me
      I will
For how long
      As long as you need
Will someone care
      Yes, child
Are you sure
      They will in time
I'm glad you're here
      As I am
I love you
      And I love you

HOLD ON
TIGHT

JOURNAL

_____
_____
_____
_____
_____
_____
_____
_____
_____
_____
_____
_____
_____
_____
_____
_____
_____
_____
_____
_____
_____
_____
_____
_____
_____

JOURNAL

Guardian Star

You're far away from me, but I'm still looking out for you.
I chose the brightest star in the sky to watch lovingly over you.

Lift your head, look high in the sky, and find the brightest star.
That star will watch over you while you're away from me so far.

When you're feeling lonely, when you're feeling lost or blue.
Look up at that star and know that I'll always care for you.

As you watch that star, please remember and please know,
That as my love for you grows, the brighter that star will glow.

I wish there was more I could say; more that I could do.
So please know that every day I also pray for you.

Until I see your face again, until you're back with me.
Remember that I chose that star to watch over you faithfully.

BRIGHTEST STAR IN THE SKY

JOURNAL

JOURNAL

_____

_____

_____

_____

_____

_____

_____

_____

_____

_____

_____

_____

_____

_____

_____

_____

_____

_____

_____

_____

_____

_____

Loneliness

The loneliness takes over, and depression fills my soul.
My body trembles with deep sobs; I feel I have no control.

I slowly sink to the floor and curl into a tight ball.
I need someone to help me, but have no strength to call.

My tears flow freely, one by one, forming a puddle on the floor.
I cry from the hurt and anguish until I can cry no more.

The cold tile chills my body, but still I do not move.
The whole world seems hopeless, and I don't know what to do.

I wonder if I just lie here, slowly dying alone.
Will anyone wonder where I am, will anyone care that I'm gone?

LONELINESS TAKES OVER

JOURNAL

_____
_____
_____
_____
_____
_____
_____
_____
_____
_____
_____
_____
_____
_____
_____
_____
_____
_____
_____
_____
_____
_____
_____
_____

JOURNAL

_____

_____

_____

_____

_____

_____

_____

_____

_____

_____

_____

_____

_____

_____

_____

_____

_____

_____

_____

_____

_____

_____

_____

The Embrace

I had a dream of strong arms, loving me, holding me tight.
I slept peacefully, like a baby, not once fearing the night.

The solid embrace that held me was gentle, yet very strong
The world seemed a safer place in those arms all night long.

The hands that softly caressed me gently pulled me near,
keeping me close to remind me of a love precious and dear.

Fingers intertwined with mine, mine becoming lost,
in a solid grip I knew would never fail at any cost.

A hug so encompassing, we were the only two on earth,
who knew a love so rare and knew of its true worth.

A HUG SO ENCOMPASSING

JOURNAL

_____
_____
_____
_____
_____
_____
_____
_____
_____
_____
_____
_____
_____
_____
_____
_____
_____
_____
_____
_____
_____
_____
_____
_____

JOURNAL

_____

_____

_____

_____

_____

_____

_____

_____

_____

_____

_____

_____

_____

_____

_____

_____

_____

_____

_____

_____

_____

_____

_____

_____

Gratitude

Peace begins with a grateful heart,
it calms the soul in a world torn apart.

Even on the darkest night,
gratitude brings forth the light.

Remember all you have in your life,
all that you're thankful for.

Concentrate on all things wonderful,
and there will be more good in store.

GRATEFUL HEART

JOURNAL

JOURNAL

Snow

I can understand how those
　　who have never seen snow,
　　　　feel when they see it
　　for the very first time.

It doesn't look cold;
　　it doesn't look as if
　　　　it would feel like ice,
　　sometimes hard, sometimes soft.

When it sits a certain way,
　　it looks bubbly and creamy,
　　　　like shaving cream
　　that is smooth on your hand.

It looks as if you would sink
　　softly and lightly when you walk on it,
　　　　instead of crunching,
　　breaking through with each step.

Yes, I can understand
　　how they would feel;
　　　　it's like having a picture
　　of how you want something to be.

Then, when you are finally able
　　to reach out and give your picture life,
　　　　the dream of it is shattered
　　by cold reality.

BREAKING THROUGH WITH EACH STEP

JOURNAL

JOURNAL

_____

_____

_____

_____

_____

_____

_____

_____

_____

_____

_____

_____

_____

_____

_____

_____

_____

_____

_____

_____

_____

_____

_____

_____

_____

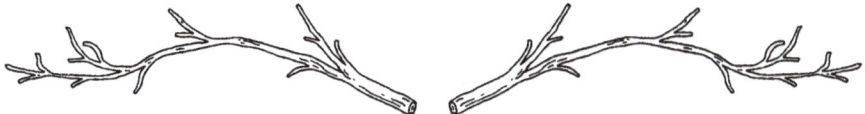

Ordinary Life

Stressful days and sleepless nights.
Painful truths cut like a knife.

Many wrongs that will never be right.
All a part of this ordinary life.

Barely getting by always a fight.
Broken families full of strife.

Endlessly searching for the light.
Welcome to this ordinary life.

ORDINARY LIFE

JOURNAL

_____

_____

_____

_____

_____

_____

_____

_____

_____

_____

_____

_____

_____

_____

_____

_____

_____

_____

_____

_____

_____

_____

_____

_____

_____

_____

_____

JOURNAL

_____
_____
_____
_____
_____
_____
_____
_____
_____
_____
_____
_____
_____
_____
_____
_____
_____
_____
_____
_____
_____
_____
_____

Castles in the Sand

We played on the beach all day, building castles in the sand.
We built a mighty kingdom in a majestic faraway land.

The prince rescued the princess, and the celebration was grand.
The king merrily approved when he knelt and asked for her hand.

What followed was the most spectacular wedding ever planned.
Then the tide came in and washed away our castles in the sand.

CASTLES IN THE SAND

JOURNAL

JOURNAL

_____

_____

_____

_____

_____

_____

_____

_____

_____

_____

_____

_____

_____

_____

_____

_____

_____

_____

_____

_____

_____

_____

_____

The Dream

One thought sparked an idea, and excitement fanned the flame.
With love it expanded and became a dream no one could tame.

Evil tried to dash those hopes like the crashing of a wave.
But courage stepped in, pushing the heart to fight and be brave.

The heart won and with this strength, a new treasure unfurled.
A reward great and wonderful, to be a gift for the entire world.

A DREAM NO ONE COULD TAME

JOURNAL

_____
_____
_____
_____
_____
_____
_____
_____
_____
_____
_____
_____
_____
_____
_____
_____
_____
_____
_____
_____
_____
_____
_____

JOURNAL

_____

_____

_____

_____

_____

_____

_____

_____

_____

_____

_____

_____

_____

_____

_____

_____

_____

_____

_____

_____

_____

_____

Adrift

I am adrift on the ocean of life, with no wind to fill my sails.

Stranded without a breeze or the strong southern gales.

I attempt to reach a distant shore, but every endeavor fails.

The void is filled with the sound of my bitter, mournful wails.

ADRIFT ON THE OCEAN OF LIFE

JOURNAL

JOURNAL

Destiny

Waiting, patiently waiting, for direction, for a sign,

Showing me my purpose, what is meant to be mine.

Darkness turns to light, as the sun begins to shine,

Revealing my true destiny, of God's own design.

DARKNESS TURNS TO LIGHT

JOURNAL

JOURNAL

Love

Love is like a red, red rose, fragile, yet strong and bold.

Nourish it and it beautifully blooms, for both young and old.

Without water, it wilts, and disappears among the thorns.

With showers, it springs back to life, the petals and leaves reborn.

Dedicating yourself, putting aside all doubts and fears.

Strengthens it at the roots, so it can bloom for many years.

LOVE IS LIKE A RED RED ROSE

JOURNAL

_____
_____
_____
_____
_____
_____
_____
_____
_____
_____
_____
_____
_____
_____
_____
_____
_____
_____
_____
_____
_____
_____
_____
_____
_____

JOURNAL

_____

_____

_____

_____

_____

_____

_____

_____

_____

_____

_____

_____

_____

_____

_____

_____

_____

_____

_____

_____

_____

_____

_____

_____

_____

Tick, Tock

My heart beats to the rhythm of the ticking of the clock
    Tick, Tock
        Tick, Tock

I become entranced and my head begins to rock
    Tick, Tock
        Tick, Tock

I watch the pendulum swing and my thoughts begin to stir
    Tick, Tock
        Tick, Tock

My mind begins to wander and the night becomes a blur
    Tick, Tock
        Tick, Tock

My heart beats faster
    Tick, Tock

My thoughts grow stronger
    Tick, Tock

My heart beats louder
    Tick, Tock

My thoughts grow longer
    Tick, Tock

My heart beats to the rhythm of the ticking of the clock
    Tick, Tock
        Tick, Tock

I become entranced and my head begins to rock
    Tick, Tock
        Tick, Tock
    Tick, Tock
        Tick, Tock
    Tick, Tock
        Tick, Tock

MY HEART BEATS FASTER TICK TOCK

JOURNAL

_____

_____

_____

_____

_____

_____

_____

_____

_____

_____

_____

_____

_____

_____

_____

_____

_____

_____

_____

_____

_____

_____

_____

_____

_____

_____

_____

JOURNAL

No Man's Land

Stuck in no man's land, the air is so dry.
Water is so scarce, I have no tears to cry.

Dust settles on me, grit sticks in my teeth.
What isn't buried in sand is buried in grief.

I cannot speak, with no breath to spare.
The road out is blocked, leading nowhere.

I hide in the dark, my back to the wind.
The storm whips around and beats me again.

It grows, stealing the remaining sunlight.
I give in to the darkness, losing the fight.

STUCK IN NO MAN'S LAND

JOURNAL

JOURNAL

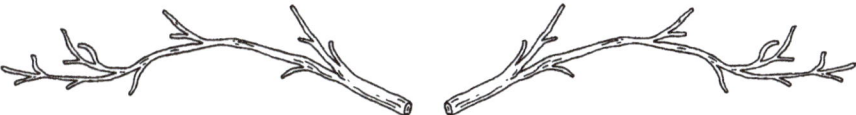

Spontaneous

He said, be spontaneous, make life wonderful and grand.
I'll lead you through the fire, take a risk and hold my hand.

My body shook with excitement and fear of the unknown.
I breathed through the panic that chilled me to the bone.

I stepped into the flames, and they sparked and started to burn.
Then the heat soothed the aches that made my broken heart yearn.

I released all that held me back as the fire set me free.
And my eyes opened in wonder to all the things that I could be.

THE FIRE
SET ME FREE

JOURNAL

JOURNAL

_____

_____

_____

_____

_____

_____

_____

_____

_____

_____

_____

_____

_____

_____

_____

_____

_____

_____

_____

_____

_____

_____

Bloom

Follow the sun to where the flowers bloom,
then play until you meet your inner child.

Relive the days of innocence and wonder,
of wandering free, exhilarated, and wild.

Bask in the beauty and cleanse your mind,
until your worries and troubles fade away.

Shake off any regret, anguish, and shame,
and forgive others for what they might say.

Let the purity of nature flow through you,
and soak into every muscle and nerve,

A beautiful new life starts for you this day,
full of the freedom and joy you deserve.

WHERE THE
FLOWERS
BLOOM

JOURNAL

_____

_____

_____

_____

_____

_____

_____

_____

_____

_____

_____

_____

_____

_____

_____

_____

_____

_____

_____

_____

_____

_____

_____

_____

_____

JOURNAL

A Single Tear

I watch you start to smile as she walks up to you.
You take her arm in arm as she smiles brightly back at you.

I see your body slightly tremble from the excitement of this day.
My body trembles also, but from love gone astray.

The vows are lovingly spoken, gently and soft.
My soul cries knowing that she has won all that I have lost.

When you put that lingering kiss upon her lips, I feel weak.
And I face a lonely world as a single tear rolls down my cheek.

YOU TAKE HER ARM IN ARM

JOURNAL

_____

_____

_____

_____

_____

_____

_____

_____

_____

_____

_____

_____

_____

_____

_____

_____

_____

_____

_____

_____

_____

_____

_____

_____

_____

JOURNAL

_____

_____

_____

_____

_____

_____

_____

_____

_____

_____

_____

_____

_____

_____

_____

_____

_____

_____

_____

_____

_____

_____

_____

_____

Wondering

I'm wondering if you need me
at all like I need you.
I'm wondering if you feel
the same emotions that I do.

Does your heart pound wildly in your chest
when you hear my name?
Does your body burn from wanting me,
and you can't extinguish the flame?

I'm wondering if you're longing
for a love like mine that's true.
I'm wondering if you love me
the way that I love you.

A LOVE THAT'S TRUE

JOURNAL

JOURNAL

_____

_____

_____

_____

_____

_____

_____

_____

_____

_____

_____

_____

_____

_____

_____

_____

_____

_____

_____

_____

_____

_____

_____

_____

Late at Night

Late at night I toss and turn,
From dreams of longing and hearts that yearn,
Of unquenched desire and fires that burn,
Of damaged souls that never learn.

Late at night I dream of a place,
That is bathed in light and full of grace,
Where lonely hearts find a warm embrace,
Where good souls always win the race.

Late at night I cannot fall asleep,
I pray the Lord my soul to keep,
To dry my tears when I weep,
To give me wings when I leap.

Late at night there is no sound,
I walk alone on hallowed ground,
I now am free, no longer bound,
I once was lost, but now am found.

ONCE WAS LOST NOW AM FOUND

JOURNAL

_____

_____

_____

_____

_____

_____

_____

_____

_____

_____

_____

_____

_____

_____

_____

_____

_____

_____

_____

_____

_____

_____

_____

JOURNAL

The Great Lady

It is a beacon in the harbor, a light upon the shore.
Beckoning to the weary, the frightened, and the poor.

With privilege, I've stood at her feet and read the parchment in her hand.
I've looked out across the threshold that welcomes all to this great land.

I have read the names on the list of those who traveled here.
Searching for their freedom, escaping past tyranny and fear.

Thankful for the opportunity, they worked day and night.
They struggled to build new lives, never giving up the fight.

They realized their goals and dreams in the land of the free.
They became a shining example of what all of us could be.

But the light that guided them here is now weak and dim.
Her crown has lost its shimmer and her smile is now grim.

Her parchment is fading, the words are harder to read.
Her dress is ragged and stained from a broken heart that bleeds.

Freedom fuels her light that shines across the shore.
Hope gives her strength to hold open the welcoming door.

As freedom and hope are lost, she is shaken to her core.
Soon she will weaken and kneel and the door will be open no more.

We must protect the great lady, to protect what is just and right.
She stood for our freedom and values, and now we must fight.

Gather now, all who were born here or beckoned here by fate.
Battle for the rights bestowed to you before it is too late.

Stand at her feet, look up at the light, and hold high your hand.
Remember what she stood for, for it is your turn to take a stand.

A LIGHT UPON THE SHORE

JOURNAL

_____
_____
_____
_____
_____
_____
_____
_____
_____
_____
_____
_____
_____
_____
_____
_____
_____
_____
_____
_____
_____
_____
_____
_____
_____

JOURNAL

_____
_____
_____
_____
_____
_____
_____
_____
_____
_____
_____
_____
_____
_____
_____
_____
_____
_____
_____
_____
_____
_____
_____
_____
_____
_____

Down

The world gets me down, and I wonder why.
I want to laugh, but only manage to cry.

I put on a brave face to hide all my pain.
The ruse leaves me lost with nothing to gain.

I'm so alone, and my future looks bleak.
I want to be strong, but I feel so weak.

The days pass me by as I tire and grow old.
I want a new life, yet I'm not that bold.

I pray for strength and the hope of tomorrow.
For love to replace my pain and my sorrow.

I PRAY FOR STRENGTH

JOURNAL

_____
_____
_____
_____
_____
_____
_____
_____
_____
_____
_____
_____
_____
_____
_____
_____
_____
_____
_____
_____
_____
_____
_____
_____

JOURNAL

For Sale

For Sale:
The broken pieces of my heart,
that need a little mending.

The Price:
The bond of your loving heart,
that is strong and neverending.

THE BOND OF YOUR LOVING HEART

JOURNAL

_____

_____

_____

_____

_____

_____

_____

_____

_____

_____

_____

_____

_____

_____

_____

_____

_____

_____

_____

_____

_____

_____

_____

_____

_____

JOURNAL

Night Thoughts

It's all so strange, these things I feel.
They're so confusing. Are they for real?

I lie awake, I cannot sleep.
I become sad, I begin to weep.

Then I am happy, the sadness gone.
I dream of life, a beautiful song.

In wonderment, I watch the stars.
They're all so bright, but away so far.

The moon is next, it fills my interest.
A feeling of love rises in my breast.

Now I am crying, I cannot cease.
The beautiful world is filled with grief.

Then all at once, my strength is spent.
These feelings are leaving, I become unbent.

I lie back down and enter another place.
Sleep is good, I wear a smile on my face.

I WATCH THE STARS

JOURNAL

_____
_____
_____
_____
_____
_____
_____
_____
_____
_____
_____
_____
_____
_____
_____
_____
_____
_____
_____
_____
_____
_____
_____

JOURNAL

Face the Night Alone

I face the night
    alone
        wondering…
            why I feel this way.
It was not right
    it couldn't have been
        or we'd be together
            together…
                right now.
Instead of alone
    facing the night
        the lonely night…
            without one another.
But we lie
    alone
        each with the same thoughts
            the same dream…
                to be together again.
Our arms
    once wrapped around each other
        are cold…
            longing to be held
                held that same way
                    once again.
Our lips burn
    burn…
        remembering how
            they once kissed.
But we do not sate
    our desires
        instead…
We insist
    we insist…
        on facing the night alone.

FACING THE
NIGHT ALONE

JOURNAL

_____

_____

_____

_____

_____

_____

_____

_____

_____

_____

_____

_____

_____

_____

_____

_____

_____

_____

_____

_____

_____

_____

_____

_____

_____

JOURNAL

Him

The darkness of the night envelops me
    I hear him.

The sounds of the night surround me
    I see him.

The coolness of the wind sweeps by me
    I'm near him.

Stars scatter across the night sky
    I feel him.

The dawn breaks through the darkness
    I lose him.

The coolness of the morning hits me
    I miss him.

I'M NEAR HIM

JOURNAL

JOURNAL

_____
_____
_____
_____
_____
_____
_____
_____
_____
_____
_____
_____
_____
_____
_____
_____
_____
_____
_____
_____
_____
_____
_____
_____
_____
_____
_____
_____

Our Movie

I want to make a movie of my memories,
of all the times I've shared with you.
I want to capture every moment,
all the things that we've been through.

Each smile, laugh and conversation
holds a special place in my heart.
Every moment is unique and special,
there's no splitting them apart.

They belong somewhere besides
the dark recesses of my mind.
To make our extraordinary history
so much easier for us to find.

And when we're old and gray
and our memories start to fade away.
We'll play our movie and remember
like it was only yesterday.

CAPTURE
EVERY
MOMENT

MEMORIES

OUR

MOVIE

JOURNAL

JOURNAL

_____

_____

_____

_____

_____

_____

_____

_____

_____

_____

_____

_____

_____

_____

_____

_____

_____

_____

_____

_____

_____

_____

_____

_____

Crying in the Dark

Crying in the dark, sad, confused and alone.
Struggling to find my way, but my life is not my own.

I pray and I fight, but the world beats me down.
The dreams I held high are shattered on the ground.

I search the inner me, looking for a new spark.
Until then, I hide alone, crying in the dark.

CRYING IN THE DARK

JOURNAL

_____
_____
_____
_____
_____
_____
_____
_____
_____
_____
_____
_____
_____
_____
_____
_____
_____
_____
_____
_____
_____
_____
_____
_____

JOURNAL

Worth

The sun's glow reflects warmly on the water,
as evening settles over the earth.

I reflect on God's grace and abundance,
and rejoice over my true worth.

GRACE AND ABUNDANCE

JOURNAL

_____
_____
_____
_____
_____
_____
_____
_____
_____
_____
_____
_____
_____
_____
_____
_____
_____
_____
_____
_____
_____
_____

JOURNAL

Inside These Walls

Inside these walls lies a power; inside these walls lies a gift.
Given to a boy a century ago, an answer to a child's wish.

The boy soon became a man, the power grew stronger each day.
With his magic he ruled a kingdom; the power showed him the way.

One fair day the man was married, to a woman who stole his heart.
When he shared his amazing gift with her, her fear tore their love apart.

Before she could escape the man, and the power of his lair.
She bore the man a healthy son; her love for him kept her there.

Then one sad day she found her son, alone in his room with the man.
The boy was granted the special gift, as he held his father's hand.

She watched the scene with a heavy heart, and died a little that day.
With her son now holding the power, she quickly faded away.

And with her last living breath, she cursed the man and his son.
Sadness lied ahead for them, and every male heir to come.

She cursed them all with sorrow, with loneliness, sadness and grief.
She stole their chances for true love; the woman died a thief.

With each curse that's made in anger, lies a way for it to be broken.
A power of the Heaven's above, a gift from them; a token.

One day a woman would come, who possessed a generous soul.
She would break the lonely spell and make the kingdom whole.

Her heart would hold no anger, her eyes would show no fear.
She would take the man's hand for life and hold him precious and dear.

There would be a new beginning, because of her loving heart.
A new bond would be forged that day, that no one could tear apart.

INSIDE THESE WALLS LIES A POWER

JOURNAL

JOURNAL

_____
_____
_____
_____
_____
_____
_____
_____
_____
_____
_____
_____
_____
_____
_____
_____
_____
_____
_____
_____
_____
_____
_____
_____
_____
_____

Sadness

Sadness crept in
   stretching its sinewy arms
      deep into her soul
Its spindly fingers
   wrapped around her fragile heart
      squeezing and choking the life
         from her tired and broken vessel
Its razor-sharp nails
   sprouted and coursed through
      her boiling blood to every vein
Its malaise engulfed her
   entirety - body, heart, and soul
      drowning her in blackness and
         expelling all light from her world

HER TIRED AND BROKEN VESSEL

JOURNAL

_____

_____

_____

_____

_____

_____

_____

_____

_____

_____

_____

_____

_____

_____

_____

_____

_____

_____

_____

_____

_____

_____

_____

_____

JOURNAL

Love and Loss

Death leaves a heartache no one can heal.
Love leaves a memory no one can steal.

The joy and sadness are hard to tell apart.
For both consume your body, soul, and heart.

They both leave you aching deep in your core.
Harboring all emotion and longing for more.

The difference is that one fills you with grief.
The other with bliss that is all too brief.

A MEMORY NO ONE CAN STEAL

JOURNAL

JOURNAL

Night

On the edge of the city, in the dark of night.

I quiet the noise and turn off the light.

I slip into bed and tuck myself in tight.

And suddenly, all with the world is right.

ALL WITH THE WORLD IS RIGHT

JOURNAL

JOURNAL

American Dream

Stripes that shimmer and shine
Stars that sparkle and gleam
Colors that never fade
Built the American Dream

Billowing in the wind
Glowing in a sunbeam
Promising freedom for all
Protecting the American Dream

AMERICAN DREAM

# JOURNAL

_____

_____

_____

_____

_____

_____

_____

_____

_____

_____

_____

_____

_____

_____

_____

_____

_____

_____

_____

_____

_____

_____

_____

_____

JOURNAL

Lonely in a Room Full of People

I sit here, away from the crowd
      yet in it
They surround me, yet I am alone
      lonely,
            in a room full of people.
I see them, and I know they're near
      yet they're far away
They talk and laugh, I know they do
      but all I hear is
            silence.
I look at the happy, smiling faces
      yet they are a blur
They dance and move around the room
      but I see it
            in slow motion.
They look at me, I see their eyes
      but they're looking past me
They walk my way, closer and closer
      but then,
            pass me by.
I sit here, away from the crowd
      yet in it
They surround me, yet I am alone
      Lonely,
            in a room full of people.

THE HAPPY SMILING FACES

JOURNAL

_____

_____

_____

_____

_____

_____

_____

_____

_____

_____

_____

_____

_____

_____

_____

_____

_____

_____

_____

_____

_____

_____

_____

_____

_____

_____

JOURNAL

Drowning

I'm drowning
      falling deeper and deeper
            into a cold sea
I'm smothering
      their faces...
            voices...
                  words...
Confusing me
      frightening me
            I don't know what to do
I'm lost
      I can't find my way up
            only down...
I'm drowning
      why won't somebody save me?

INTO A
COLD SEA

JOURNAL

_____
_____
_____
_____
_____
_____
_____
_____
_____
_____
_____
_____
_____
_____
_____
_____
_____
_____
_____
_____
_____
_____
_____
_____
_____
_____

JOURNAL

The Lighthouse

I stand proudly on the shore, sending out a beacon of light.
Encouraging ships tossed by the sea to not give up the fight.

I guide them in the darkness, helping to bring them home.
Promising them safe harbor, so they no longer need to roam.

When the sea calls to them again, I help them find their way.
When the next journey ends, I'll lead them back again one day.

GUIDE IN THE DARKNESS

 JOURNAL

_____
_____
_____
_____
_____
_____
_____
_____
_____
_____
_____
_____
_____
_____
_____
_____
_____
_____
_____
_____
_____
_____
_____
_____

JOURNAL

_____
_____
_____
_____
_____
_____
_____
_____
_____
_____
_____
_____
_____
_____
_____
_____
_____
_____
_____
_____
_____
_____
_____

The Wolf at the Door

The wolf at the door howled, scavenging for its next meal.
It scratched and tore at the lock, fighting to break the seal.

The woman inside stood strong, courageously guarding her heart.
But the wolf broke through at midnight, tearing her home apart.

The woman cowered in the corner through the terrifying night.
As the wolf savagely plundered, devouring everything in sight.

When all else was gone, the wolf quickly turned her way.
Its eyes glazed and it foamed at the mouth, examining its prey.

The woman cried out for help, praying all was not lost.
She stood tall, exposing herself, knowing what that might cost.

The wolf lunged and she plunged her broken cross into its side.
The wolf yelped and crawled away, looking for a place to hide.

The woman, much stronger now, chased the wolf far away.
Dawn broke through the darkness, bringing with it a brand new day.

THE WOLF AT THE DOOR HOWLED

JOURNAL

_____

_____

_____

_____

_____

_____

_____

_____

_____

_____

_____

_____

_____

_____

_____

_____

_____

_____

_____

_____

_____

_____

_____

_____

_____

JOURNAL

Nothingness

The night is deathly quiet
Silence fills the air.
I hear only my imagination
A sound that is not there.

I sit alone in darkness
There is no light that I can see.
My eyes strain to see a shadow
But my sight has abandoned me.

I reach out to feel for something
Someone who is not there.
But my hands have no feeling
There is nothingness everywhere.

My nose wrinkles in anticipation
But I cannot smell.
I imagine the scent of roses
But I can't remember very well.

My senses have all left me
I only have my mind.
But I know that it too will leave me
It's only a matter of time.

I cannot laugh or smile
I cannot make myself cry.
Nothingness fills my being
I cannot feel, although I try.

I'm empty, drained of everything
But I know I'm here.
I would be afraid, if only I could
But I cannot fear.

I KNOW
I'M HERE

JOURNAL

JOURNAL

Glimmer of Light

At midnight, on your worst day, when the world is pitch black,
and you wonder if you'll see the light of day.

Agony and heartbreak have become your two best friends,
for joy and fulfillment seem too far away.

Don't give in to the temptation of slipping into the abyss,
assuming that the silence will bring you peace.

That void holds nothing but disappointment and anguish,
for the misery in that pit will never cease.

Hold on tight, instead, to the promise of prayer and hope,
peer into the deepest recesses of the night.

That faith will break through the darkness and the gloom,
and that crack will reveal a glimmer of light.

GLIMMER OF LIGHT

JOURNAL

_____
_____
_____
_____
_____
_____
_____
_____
_____
_____
_____
_____
_____
_____
_____
_____
_____
_____
_____
_____
_____
_____
_____

JOURNAL

The House Down on the Street

At the house down the street, the lights never come on,
at night, the windows are dark.
No one opens the old-fashioned doors
or walks in the wide lonely rooms.

The paint on the house is withered and worn,
its color is unknown to the eye.
A few of the windows have been broken and boarded,
giving the house a look of doom.

An old rusty trike sits on the sidewalk outside,
beside it, a faded worn ball.
Where are the children who played with those toys?
Their laughter echoes in my mind.

The flowers that once bloomed are now brown and stiff,
they crackle at a touch of the hand.
The wooden-built sandbox is now broken and old,
the sand as hard as frozen soil.

At the house down the street where the lights cease to shine,
I stand and look beyond.
I see the family of four eating their dinner,
they talk and laugh out loud.

The television is on, though no one is watching,
bringing a little noise to the quiet room.
The floors are spotless, the windows sparkle,
the furniture catches the light.

But before me stands only an old lonely house,
a secret hidden behind its doors.
And no one will ever know, for the only key
lies cold within my heart.

WITHERED AND WORN

JOURNAL

_____
_____
_____
_____
_____
_____
_____
_____
_____
_____
_____
_____
_____
_____
_____
_____
_____
_____
_____
_____
_____
_____
_____
_____
_____

JOURNAL

The Whispering of the Wind

I hear the whining of the wind through my window
It carries and whispers a story of days gone by.

I listen carefully to what it cries and I shudder
The wind is known to change but never lie.

At night it reaches cool fingers in to touch me
I awake with a cold sweat upon my brow.

For it left me with yet another scary secret
I am frightened, although I'll be all right for now.

I lie awake and await the coming of the dawn
Or will the dawn shine upon me this day?

The wind told of all the misery to come soon
But when it would happen it did not say.

As the sun breaks through the darkness I sit in wonder
For another one like it will never again light my skies.

For when I turn to look in the other direction
I see the mighty storm on the rise.

AWAIT THE COMING OF THE DAWN

JOURNAL

JOURNAL

The Mighty Oak

At winter's first strike
The mighty oak sheds its leaves
But always stands strong

It wakes in the spring
Returning to its glory
Steady and graceful

RETURNING TO ITS GLORY

JOURNAL

JOURNAL

The Final Call

There is a sound; what is it I heard?
    For the wind carries it away.

Is it a cry? No, my ears deceive me.
    He will not come today.

The darkness surrounds me, my heart grows weary.
    Is the moment near?

Will I now be alone forever?
    Will I lose what I hold dear?

Or will it be easy, this time for me?
    Will I live in a happier place?

Will I live in wonder, and dream sweet dreams,
    That will bring a smile to my face?

I can't help but wonder, even though it brings fear,
    But I will not wonder anymore.

For it was not the wind that I heard this time,
    But the call I've been waiting for.

I WILL NOT WONDER ANYMORE

JOURNAL

_____
_____
_____
_____
_____
_____
_____
_____
_____
_____
_____
_____
_____
_____
_____
_____
_____
_____
_____
_____
_____
_____
_____
_____
_____

JOURNAL

My Heart Belongs to You

One night while I was sleeping, love, I had a dream of you.
You came to me and kissed me sweet, and left me wanting you.

And so I chased you through the realms, of my wondrous dream.
You evaded me, but I caught you dear, and held you close to me.

For your heart belongs to me love, as mine belongs to you.
I swear you'll never leave my side, until this life is through.

But then one day you ran away, and took your love from me.
I searched for you from far to near, over mountains and raging seas.

And so I found you once again, crying on a hill.
You had not left me after all, but were taken against your will.

For your heart belongs to me love, as mine belongs to you.
I swear you'll never leave my side, until this life is through.

But then I noticed your blue eyes, shining oh so bright.
You then unfolded those silver wings, and blinded me with your light.

I fell to my knees and held my head, this could not be true.
You were the only one I loved, now what would I do?

For your heart belongs to me love, as mine belongs to you.
I swore you'd never leave my side, until this life is through.

You held me to your chest then, held me oh so tight.
You kissed me sweetly one last time, then left me in the night.

And now I sit alone love, and wait for your return.
I weep, I sob and tremble dear, and my heart achingly yearns.

But you do not come back to me, I alone live through the years.
All I have left to my name, are your memories and my tears.

Your heart still belongs to me love, as mine belongs to you.
But you have left my side, dear, and now my life is through.

MY HEART BELONGS TO YOU

JOURNAL

_____
_____
_____
_____
_____
_____
_____
_____
_____
_____
_____
_____
_____
_____
_____
_____
_____
_____
_____
_____
_____
_____
_____
_____
_____
_____
_____
_____

JOURNAL

The Phoenix

Burning, tremendous burning,
    scorching from the inside out.

Thick smoke, blinding blackness,
    heaviness choking the airway.

Deep pain, intense and extreme,
    melting the heart and soul.

Powerful will, survival is a must,
    strength pounding through every vein.

Fighting, overcoming,
    refusing to give in to the agony.

Clawing, digging a way
    through the heavy soot and gritty ashes.

Surfacing, gasping for air,
    shaking away the embers.

Gulping, deep breaths of oxygen,
    morphing death into life.

Rising again as a new bird, a phoenix so strong,
    nothing can burn it again.

MORPHING DEATH INTO LIFE

JOURNAL

_____
_____
_____
_____
_____
_____
_____
_____
_____
_____
_____
_____
_____
_____
_____
_____
_____
_____
_____
_____
_____
_____
_____
_____
_____

JOURNAL

_____
_____
_____
_____
_____
_____
_____
_____
_____
_____
_____
_____
_____
_____
_____
_____
_____
_____
_____
_____
_____
_____
_____

Connect with Ann

http://www.anncknickell.com

https://linktr.ee/anncknickell

www.ingramcontent.com/pod-product-compliance
Lightning Source LLC
Chambersburg PA
CBHW051613120626
46551CB00014B/1778